Saving America

FOR OUR CHILDREN AND GRANDCHILDREN

Francis Michael Del Vecchio

authorHOUSE®

AuthorHouse™
1663 Liberty Drive
Bloomington, IN 47403
www.authorhouse.com
Phone: 1-800-839-8640

First published by AuthorHouse   3/18/2011

ISBN: 978-1-4567-4385-7 (e)
ISBN: 978-1-4567-4384-0 (dj)
ISBN: 978-1-4567-4383-3 (sc)

Library of Congress Control Number: 2011902996

Printed in the United States of America

Any people depicted in stock imagery provided by Thinkstock are models, and such images are being used for illustrative purposes only. Certain stock imagery © Thinkstock.

This book is printed on acid-free paper.

Because of the dynamic nature of the Internet, any web addresses or links contained in this book may have changed since publication and may no longer be valid. The views expressed in this work are solely those of the author and do not necessarily reflect the views of the publisher, and the publisher hereby disclaims any responsibility for them.

FIXING AMERICA FOR OUR GRANDCHILDREN

I'm not a writer so I don't give a damn if you read this book. It is a book to my grand children and everyone in their age group. This book is what I think and feel regardless of what is broadcast on radio, TV, internet and in the written media. The day will come when you will look for the book and want to know what grandpa would have done. That will be right after you curse out the older generation for getting you into this fiscal and political mess in the first place. So keep it handy for an interesting quick read from an intriguing old man. If you are naive and wait for the other person to do something, stop reading now, you haven't faced the reality of life yet and you still depend on Mommy and Daddy for help. You missed some lessons in life or your therapist gave you some bad advice. The purpose of this book is to advise my grandchildren, the brats, as I affectionately call them and they are. Their parents want them to have all the advantages in life as I wanted for my children, but sometimes we go overboard. They never understand every thing comes with a price in this world today.

The next reason you shouldn't read this book is it is not

a literary masterpiece. All the proper grammar will not be used because it comes from the heart and mind and we do not write like we speak or think, so get over it or get on with it. You will need to use the index because I write what I think and feel when I want, no particular order. It will be a reference for them to look back on and really get to know their grandpa. Right now they could care less what grandpa thinks unless they need some specific advice on how to get around their mother and father and I am always willing to do that. So, Angelica, Alexis, Michael, Michael and Anthony get ready for this ride, for the life you face isn't going to be a pleasant one based on the direction we are currently going. You guessed it, Pop Pop is going to lecture you on life and politics and you better take heed. I know you don't give a damn now because everything is going your way, but you must realize the magic age of independence and paying more than your fair share is getting closer everyday. You will learn how greedy my generation and your parents generation were and the cost to you will be staggering. We all want to do for our children, but we are actually doing it to them.

PEOPLE WILL DO TO YOU WHAT YOU LET THEM DO TO YOU. THAT INCLUDES YOUR GOVERNMENT AND YOU WILL CURSE US FOR IT AND HAVE EVERY RIGHT TO DO SO, BECAUSE WE HAVE DONE IT TO YOU.

SO, THIS IS WHAT YOU GET FOR COMPLAINING THAT GRANDPA IS TALKING POLITICS ALL THE TIME AND YOUR TO DUMB TO LISTEN, PARTICIPATE OR ASK QUESTIONS.

Let's be clear from the beginning, there is nothing wrong with America. It's the dumb asses that think they know what's right that are the problem. The next problem are the dummies who vote for them because they are handsome or pretty and speak well. They make you feel good while they empty your wallets. So the nature of this book that I struggle through is simple, get involved, become knowledgeable, or take it hard on the chin. YOUR CHOICE, MAKE IT A GOOD ONE.

BORN IN AMERICA, SO WHAT ARE YOU?

You were born in America so what is the problem with being American. I was born here and I am an American. I am not an Italian American even though my parents were Italian and someone forgot to tell them they were born in America. Their parents were born in Italy and they were Italian Americans. Because I like pasta and pizza doesn't makes me an Italian American it make me and American who likes pasta and pizza. I would like it no matter what country I was in. What you need to know is the people in foreign countries have it right, they hate you because your American and they like you because your American. When you are in another country they ask if you are American, not Italian American or Black American or Polish American. Get it, they have it right.

ONLY IN AMERICA WE CAN'T GET IT RIGHT.

You need to be a prefix like Italian, Irish, Spanish, African or whatever. Well that is not the way it is, you are Americans. Your as American as the first people who were born here, who ever they were. The only problem is they never knew that till the government told them they live in the United States

5

of America, they still think they are Indians. They might be because they are treated differently and have different rights in a country were all people are suppose to be equal. Figure it out for yourself, I'm still confused.

NO COMMON LANGUAGE OR HERITAGE

This is one reason we can't get it right, we have no official language and these pussies in Washington haven't figured it out in over four hundred years. The forefathers couldn't get it together either, but make no mistake about it and don't let the labels on the boxes confuse you, we speak English or some form of it. We have no point of origin to start from. You are not required to learn English. The politicians want to keep Americans diversified. It is easier to deal with a segmented group than to do what is right for all Americans. They do not think of America first and never be fooled by their rhetoric. They always speak about their constituents. I never saw that mentioned in the Constitution. What is the first thing we need, IDENTITY, A COMMON LANGUAGE, if you can't converse with the rest of the nation you may as well crawl in a box and close it. You were born in the greatest country in the world and if you don't think so then visit a third world country. They did vote on a language over two hundred years ago and German lost by one vote, so they let it go and it has caused complications ever since and we still can't get it right.

Commonality is a trait everyone tends to draw to, a good example, is during a disaster everyone help and draws together but we never continue that common thread because we all think we are someone or something else. We all forget we are AMERICANS. We move back to our comfort zone and neighborhoods.

WHO BELONGS IN AMERICA

People who want to be Americans, sounds simple, not so. Most people come here for what they can get and not give. Others come because they are greedy and will take advantage. Others just want to work and that's okay providing they want to be Americans and not users of the freedoms this country provides. People that just want to work here ought to find work in their own country. Can't find work there so change it, not America. Sending our money abroad is not the answer. Working and living here is the answer. Paying taxes here is the answer. Working underground is not the answer. There are some that say we can't get along without the migrant workers, that's wrong. We must improve our technology and treat our workers with respect and move in their shoes to achieve this. We have to give a worker a reason to stay and live a good life in America. So, how can we do this?

Control the boarders and shut them down till we get a handle on the people here illegally. Find them and give them an option, study the language, pass a basic intelligence test, and pay a fine through hirer social security taxes. Is this fair? It would be a start. Something has to be done. People who have criminal records should be sent back. We have enough of our own. They will have a six month period to declare themselves and after that they will be deported. You will not have to support people that aren't helping to support America.

The people that want to hold on to their heritage, go home, we want them to be happy and stop making our life miserable. Commonality just might help eliminate some of the prejudice we have toward each other. Closing the borders is not a bad thing to do. Getting control is a good and right thing to do. All the other countries do it. So if you really want to be of another nationality, go home and BE HAPPY.

All the festivals we have in this country for other nationalities are a dumping ground to sell junk and food. We must celebrate our own existence and that is it. I have a sense of pride when we get together for the Forth of July. It has relative meaning and many settlers and pioneers lost their life securing home rule and freedom. This country should be proud of its accomplishments and celebrate, celebrate, dance to the music, not apologize for who we are and what we have done.

The world looked to us as an example of freedom. They admired our standard of living and that is why they come here, but they need to remember that they should assimilate and begin a new life not bring there short comings and expect us to accept them as part of this society. They left for a better opportunity and situation for their family so get with the program. People do not have to forget their past but they need to live in the present. The world has proven over and over again, different cultures can't live together, someone always wants to be dominant. America should dominate and we should want to be Americans.

THE AMERICAN FLAG

This is the symbol of our country here and abroad. I don't think it was the intent of the founders to piss on, shit on, or burn the flag. There isn't a clause in the constitution that gives you the right of free expression, speech you dumb ass judges, expressions are important for people who can't speak. They should wrap the judges who voted affirmatively in the flag and set them on fire. This is the one of the most ludicrous decisions I ever heard of. Is there a school for supreme court judges. They sure need one or they forgot everything they learned growing up. High intelligence is not a requirement for a justice, it certainly doesn't out weight common sense. What other country allows this nonsense. They wouldn't burn their law degree, why the flag.

We have rules for how to treat the flag, hang it, display it, wrap it and destroy it when it becomes tattered. We do not have a rule for burning it just because you don't like what it stands for. Much blood has flowed and many lives have been lost protecting what it stands for.

From the Revolutionary War through the Civil War and the World Wars, that flag has set more people free and saved many lives through its' generosity than all the nations combined. It has faced every challenge with ferocious conviction and still garners respect throughout the world. Freedom comes at a price, not from ashes but from the blood and pride of a nation.

LOVE IT, LEAVE IT, OR BURN YOUR OWN ASS NOT THE "AMERICAN FLAG."

THE CONSTITUTION OF THE UNITED STATES OF AMERICA

The Declaration of Independence was the promise, the Constitution was the fulfillment. So, what happened. They stopped working, no, they stopped keeping their promises. Mans' solemn word of trust has disintegrated over time. Giving your word meant something at one time. That was all you needed to create a bond of integrity, faith and loyalty, now you need ten reams of paper and a lawyer to go with it and even that isn't good enough sometimes.

What do children really know about the Constitution? What they need to know is it doesn't say the government will take care of you for the rest of your life. I think they grow up with that idea until they hit the workforce, then most of them learn what responsibility is all about. I blame most of it on the old adage, Don't mix Politics and Religion, and to that extreme it isn't discussed. The people who do discuss it run the country.

The bottom line is simple, we have a Constitution that every politician swears to uphold and none of them do. There isn't a governing body to police the behavior and performance of the congress and the senate or the president. They police themselves and give themselves a raise whenever they want. There needs to be a civilian review board to monitor this calamity. The more the government gives you the more they will take from you and tell you what to do. They in essence will become your mommy and daddy and, the term, because I said so will prevail. Read the damn Constitution and open your mind, it is not a social document.

RECAP TIME

Just like you were in school, I will recap what your little brains need to remember. This will help you get through life and set you on a path of self respect and total responsibility. Right now your biggest challenge is getting up in the morning, what are your friends doing, what's on face book, did I get any text messages while I slept, and what electronic things should I play with today, and don't forget to brush your teeth.

1. Respect your parents and especially your grandparents and remember they are the old fools who got you in this mess.

2. Intelligence does not replace common sense. As you study history you will see this over and over. You will also note we don't learn very well from the past history and it is obvious.

3. Don't forget that you are Americans and be proud of it.

4. Your heritage is your family and the traditions you set. Don't worry about what your ancestors did, they are dead. Don't follow their mistakes including the ones I made, they are numerous, but I learned from them.

5. Speak the best English you can. If you hang around

with people who swear often, then send them a dictionary for Christmas. English is the language in America, master it.

6. Respect the flag and take care of it like your favorite piece of clothing. Treat it the way you wanted to be treated. Don't let people tread on it and respect all who shed blood for it.

7. The Constitution, read it and endear the moment. So much has happened and it still stands strong. There is a good reason for that. The Constitution is the foundation for your way of life. Remember poverty breeds contempt.

8. When the founding fathers formed the constitution I doubt if they considered the jackasses that would try to use it for immoral advantages. That was an age when a mans word meant something and it still does with some individuals today. Use your common sense when you read it because I doubt it will be taught to you in school in its' pure form.

9. The constitution wasn't written with deranged people in mind. It was for the every day hard working people of their time, not the lazy bastards who take advantage of it for a free ride. Make a clear distinction between those that need help and those that help themselves and think they are entitled to a free ride. Nothing in life is free.

10. Respect yourself, respect your body, respect others and respect the fact you live in America, where one person can make a difference.

POWER TO THE PEOPLE
CONGRESS
PRESIDENT
JUSTICE SYSTEM

If you believe the power belongs to the people you are mighty mistaken. Oh, you elect the congress and the president and it is amazing how many time grown, informed adults make the same mistake. Remember I told you learn from your mistakes and don't make them again.

I believe James Carville said it best, " The voter is basically dumb and lazy. The reason I became a democratic operative instead of a republican is because there were more democrats who didn't have a clue than there were republicans." This is the sad truth. I agree that most people who vote are not informed or understand the ramifications of their ignorance. When people feel entitled they look for the government to help them and smart operatives take advantage of that, they really don't care about you.

Voting because your parents, friends, and others say it's the right thing to do without making up your own mind is dumb. If you can't make a decisive decision about the candidates then vote for yourself. This is not the answer to the problem but it will show the political parties your distain for their choices. Do not back away from your convictions and don't be afraid to voice them. The people who gave their life for that right will be proud of you. This doesn't give you a license to be off the wall, even though my views seem that way at times. You must remember, I'm Pop Pop, BE YOURSELF.

CONGRESS

There are members of congress that are intelligent and have common sense, but the majority vote with party lines and let a few people lead them. Remember, I always told you lead, follow, or get the hell out of the way, and that's the problem. They keep bumping into each other and never stand on their own.

Look at this stupidity, you run as a democrat and you vote as a democrat and the same goes for the republicans, dumb. They are elected to uphold the Constitution not the party line. They have no guts and they let a few people do their thinking for them. As a collective group they are one big asshole and we all know what comes from that. If you don't get it, sit on the toilet and see if that doesn't give you a clue.

Congress needs to be in touch with the people and the only way to do that is to have the same benefits and conditions exist.

1. Congress has its own retirement plan. They are not on social security. What is more important to them, fixing it or getting reelected.

2. They have better health benefits and pay less for them.

3. They have more vacation and leisure time and do their own daily schedule.

4. They need to show up for work everyday, missing votes is not what they get paid for.

5. They need to balance their own check book. They should not be allowed to write over drafts and they do, personally.

6. They need to eliminate ear marks, a very appropriate name for a pig.

7. All legislation should stand on its own, without attachments and addendums. MOST IMPORTANT IS KEEP IT SIMPLE FOR EVERY AMERICAN TO UNDERSTAND WHEN THEY READ IT. I would venture a guess that most congressmen don't understand most of what is written and that's why they don't read the legislation. They are lazy or dumb or BOTH. Their is no work ethic for them.

8. Congress should have a civilian review board for their rules violations. Policing themselves is dumb, stupid, ridiculous, and down right insane.

9. Congress should be given performance reviews just like the rest of Americans. Don't believe this crap that the people can vote them out, because the voting system is corrupt and does not take into account the ignorance of the voter, for example, buying votes, dead people voting, and illegal immigrants voting. This does not include the people who don't give a damn and the ones who vote the way daddy did. The review process is simple, don't spend more than you make unless it a national emergency that affects the nation and do you understand the laws they passed.

10. Congress needs to pass a simple law, you sell it here then you better make it or assemble here. They need to put America First.

11. Congress should have term limits and retirement requirements.

12. Congress should not be allowed to pass their own pay increase.

13. All criminal behavior should have an automatic doubling of sentence. The sentence should be as directed without mitigating circumstances.

14. All congressional seats should be recallable by their constituents according to predetermined guidelines, i.e., broken promises in their control.

HOW DOES COMGRESS WORK ACTUALLY IT DOESN'T

1. This is the way it is suppose to work, the bill is delivered to the house and dropped into the Hopper, a wooden box on the clerks desk. The clerk assigns it a number and it is reviewed by the speaker and sent to the committee for review and its chances of passing are determined. This is horse shit. The fact is it will never get to committee if the speaker doesn't like it because it will never be assigned or it will go to committee and if they don't act on it the bill is dead. So what do we have here kiddies, you have the most powerful person in government deciding what will or will not become law. Why are they the most powerful? SIMPLE, ONLY CONGRESS CAN SPEND MONEY AND THE OLD ADAGE OF, MONEY TALKS AND BULLSHIT WALKS, IS VERY TRUE. The President can recommend and influence congress on bills, so he is the bullshit part of this equation.

2. If the bill gets to committee, they decide the fate of the bill. They can send it to the subcommittee for

further investigation. If they take no action the bill is dead.   3. The subcommittee holds hearings and all appropriate supporters and objectors can testify and record their views.

3. The subcommittee will review all the findings and MARKUP the bill as they call it. This means they will amend and change the bill before they send it back to full committee. If they vote not to report legislation the bill dies.

4. The full committee reviews the subs findings and votes on its recommendations. If it passes the bill moves on, if not the bill dies.

5. Somewhere in the next process the chamber or entire house will review, reject, or amend the bill. I understood that to be all 435 members of the house will do this, GOOD LUCK, that is not the case. This is only if they make so many changes they reassign the bill a new number and it is considered a new bill. The bill is passed to the whole chamber and voted on. If it passes it will be sent to the senate chamber where it goes through the same process. So, 435 representatives vote and pass a bill and send it to 100 senators who will follow a similar process.

6. The chamber or senate may approve, reject, change or ignore the bill. If they approve it, the bill goes to the president, change it, the conference committee will review it, reject or ignore it and it is dead. So, 100 senators will send a message of screw you or halleluiah. Maybe a lot of work and money for nothing.

7. The conference committee made up of senators

and representatives will review the bill and try to come to a compromise, if not, the bill is dead. If they agree on terms it goes back to the house and senate for approval. At this point it will go to the President.

8. The president can signs it the bill becomes law. If the president takes no action while congress is in session it becomes law. If the president takes no action after congress has adjourned the second session it is a pocket veto and is dead. The president can veto it right away and it goes back to congress.

9. He congress has the right to override the veto with a 2/3rds majority of the house and senate and it will become law, if not, it is dead.

So, BRATS, this is the process for passing bills and allocating money for the government to spend. What a crock of shit and I will tell you why. A diverse nation that we are because people want to be something other than American can stop unfavorable legislation if a particular group doesn't like it. A good example is every person who works must pay some form of income tax. The poor are not going to like this or the different minority groups because they represent the poorer class. The middle class may object because they will have to carry a bigger portion of the taxes and the rich could care less because they are rich and a few dollars more is insignificant to them. If it was aimed solely at them they would bitch also. Is there an answer to this dilemma? Yes!

SIMPLE LAWS, WITH SIMPLE UNDERSTANDINGS, THAT IS FAIR TO ALL Americans. A simple law would be to Eliminate all diverse classifications off of application and registration forms. The only prevailing question should be, are you an American, yes or no. Anyone with most of their brain in tact should know if they are American born or naturalized.

Legislation is like anything else, garbage in, garbage out. Job justification for the congress is filling in the blanks and producing documents that most people don't understand. I don't think they understand it themselves.

WHAT IS LEGISLATION DESIGNED TO DO?
PROTECT YOU AND THE COUNTRY

Oh yea, it is more like they strip you of your rights and protect the criminals. These congressional people can't even decide if this is America or a conglamorate of every nation and religion in the world. They all need special rules to govern their situation, horse shit. You can't protect people unless you are all on the same field, then there would not be an issue of profiling. This is a load of crap. If we were all American then it would be considered checking out a suspicious person. That's not the way it works. The leaders of theses groups brainwash the people that they are special and need special help because of there situation in life. Their situation in life is what they make it. Everyone on this earth is human, I hope. This is where it starts and stops. I HAVE ALWAYS TOLD YOU THAT THERE ARE TWO TYPES OF PEOPLE ON THIS EARTH, GOOD ONES AND BAD ONES. Here is a good example, when a person needs help they do not pick and choose who will help them, they take it from the closest and most willing and it might be a good person or bad, most likely good.

The government that provides protection for us is our worst enemy. They insist on breaking us up in to societal groups and hang labels on us. This is promotes instant predjuice and we learn at an early age to profile. Our parents provide additional predjudices brought on by life experiences good or bad. We always tend to remember the worst first. The biggest culprit is the media and the twist they put in their stories. This promotes more predjuice. A good example is the constant referal to race, color or ancestry. The simple explaination is one American hurting another. Good versus evil and that is what it amounts to. This seems to idealistic but that is what we have allowed outside sources do to us. You repeat it long enough and loud enough and eventually they will believe it.

I could speak on this all day but what you need to remember is the government can't protect anyone. They just pass laws to punish bad behavior.

As far as protecting our country goes, we can hold our own in an all out war but we can't control our borders or keep illegal's and drugs out. We as Americans are part of the problem because we demand these things and there are enough dopes out there willing to provide us with illegals and drugs and we are the dopes on the other end. Because a certain percentage of the population wants, we all have to pay the price in money and lives. We constantly set ourselves up and expect the government to rescue us. What a joke and it's on us. You open yourself up for abuse and you will get it. So, PROTECT YOURSELF AND MAKE THE RIGHT CHOICES, DO NOT SURCUMB TO A MOMENT OR SITUATION, YOU SET THE RULES AND THE CONDITIONS.

MONEY, MONEY, AND MORE MONEY

We all like money and what it will do for us, especially you kids. Pop Pop has been generous to a fault. It is a good thing that your parents have better money management than I did at their age. You have to think like a professional gambler and remember that bankroll management and discipline are the key to SAVING, investing and spending money. The expression of follow the money is for catching criminals, measuring the effectiveness of politicians on the dumb meter, and trying to figure out how to pay the electric bill or put food on the table. Your grandmother and I were very reckless with our money until our daughter, LORI, managed our finances out of a fiscal mess. We saved, invested and spent but LORI applied the discipline and thank you for that. If you are really bad with money find help because you will never change.

You can't make a dime into a dollar and that is what the government has been trying to do as long as I can remember. Some dumb ass economists think it is good to owe money. I wonder what their portfolio looks like. I'm here to say if you can't afford it don't buy it or don't do it. Simple!

At this writing the government owes the American people and other countries about fourteen trillion dollars. That is a hell of a lot of debt, but more so it is a lot of bad spending decisions and lack of discipline and it gets worse by the day. These dumb asses can't stop spending. It is like they are impulse shopping and they have to spend money to feel good, only it's not their money they are spending. They don't understand the word balance. They think it means teter on the brink and that is where they keep us all the time.

They are a feckless bunch that is only concerned about themselves. That is a terrible thing to say but they are people who care more about votes then their own morality. They are a herd of sheep that keep moving in a circle and there isn't a leader among them willing to break that circle. They swore to protect America, not just the voters in their districts, and we are floating in a sea of debt.

There was a day when a penny or nickle actually bought something. Now I think the penny candy is a dime or more. If you think about all the taxes you pay you will probably need medication. This is a short list off the top of my head:

Federal income tax state income tax
Federal unemployment tax state unemployment tax
Medicare   state disability tax
Social security state sales tax
Federal Gasoline tax state gasoline tax
Federal tax on liquor state tax on liquor
Federal tax on cigaretts state tax on cigaretts
Federal tax on phone calls Highway tolls

The list could go on forever. The drunks in congress spend it like running water and they tax that too! So where does it end, it doesn't. Congress will continue to spend recklessly until people rebel and I'm afraid you will see that in your lifetime. The real problem when it comes to voting is they figure when the problem arises from their reckless legislation, the people that voted for this will probably be dead already. Look at medicare. Johnson added it to the civil rights bill in the sixties and under estimated its cost. This is a perfect example of you do this for me and I'll do that for you. What they really did was screw the future generations. Pop Pop could go on and on and on about this but the simple rule applies, if you don't have it don't spend it and did you really need it anyway. If you can't manage your bankroll then find someone you can trust to do it for you. I wish I would have learned that lesson early in life and it applies to everything. Seek the best advise and make the best decision.

WHO SHOULD PAY TAXES

The answer is simple, everybody and it should be fair but not equal. Poor and middle class people pay as much taxes as rich people, maybe more. A good example is we pay the same amount of tax for gas, electric, tolls, food, clothes and so on. The difference is the more you have to spend the more you pay in taxes and that doesn't seem fair, however when it comes to federal and state income taxes, it differs greatly. I firmly believe if you don't pay taxes you shouldn't be voting and telling others who do pay taxes how to spend the money. That said, everyone should pay taxes even if it is only twenty four dollars a year, no matter how poor you are.

EVERYONE WANTS TO BE TREATED EQUAL UNTIL IT COMES TO YOUR BANK ACCOUNT.

The current system is not equal. Statistically, supposedly only fifty percent of the earners pay federal income taxes. What is wrong with this picture. Why doesn't the government understand, IT'S YOUR SPENDING STUPID! What a bunch of dumb asses. ELEMENTRY, CUT SPENDING AND DO IT PROPORTIONITLY, DAH!!!!!!!!!

The system needs to be revamped and the key is simple, no matter how much you take in from the people you can't spend mor than 95% of that money. The next critical item on the agenda is the price of gas and other staple items. They must be stabilized. They have more effect on the everyday economy than all the dumb ass mistakes they make in congress. All the tax savings they are giving people are going to help them survive the everday price increases in staple items. There isn't money left to invest or save.

1. Gas goes up Food goes up
2. Gas goes up Transportation goes up
3. Gas goes up Business expenses go up, no hiring
4. Gas goes up Delivery prices increase across the board
5. Gas goes up Cost of goods goes up
6. Gas goes up Everything goes up, GET IT DAH DAH!!!!!

The list could go on forever. The point is when something goes up something goes down, like a see saw when you were little Brats. When you were up in the air you were happy, gas went up so you started on your way down and you could not stop the decent. Happy days are gone again. There are items that the government needs to control, and I'm not an advocate of government control, but this needs to be done. GASOLINE, OIL FOR HEAT, PRODUCTS THAT PRODUCE ENERGY, AND THE COST OF ENERGY. GET IT, STABELIZE THESE PRICES AND YOU CAN HAVE A REASONABLE CHANCE AT BALANCING A HOME BUDGET AND A GOVERNMENT BUDGET.

So, in the end who needs to pay taxes, EVERYONE, FROM THE DAY THEY BECOME OF LEGAL AGE. Who needs to determine how much you can spend, the balance in your check book, NOT THE LIMIT ON YOUR CREDIT CARD. That goes especially for the government.

Your great grandfather always said ," THE GOVERNMENT CAN'T GIVE YOU ANYTHING THEY DON'T TAKE AWAY FROM YOU NOW OR EVENTUALLY. YOU CAN'T MAKE A DIME INTO A DOLLAR." THE BOTTOM LINE, EVERYONE HAS TO PAY TAXES, EVERYONE!!!!!

THE MORE THEY LEGISLATE, THE MORE RIGHTS YOU GIVE UP

Do you really think we are free in America, then you must be crazy. Yes we have a level of freedom that other citizens of the world wish they had, but lets really look at the issue. The local government makes laws, the county government makes laws, the state government makes laws and the federal government makes laws. Then there is your spouse who makes laws and your boss and so on. Do you really have the freedom the pioneers were accustomed to. I doubt it. We are a regulated society and the government holds all the cards. The Supreme Court doesn't even protect our rights and ownerships. There is very little we do as people that isn't predetermined. Our decisions are steered toward work, obeying the laws and trying to be successful and good decent people, as well as good parents, sometimes too good. Disappointment never hurt anyone and we protect our children from that as much as possible, but we indebt them to the whole world for the rest of there lives. How dumb are we and the people who lead us.

A judge once told me ignorance of the law is no excuse. He never mentioned that I would need a computer in my brain to know what all the laws are. I finally woke up to that realization when I was audited by the IRS and they pointed out that I needed to cooperate. I was in a room with law books numbering in the hundreds. The agent directed my attention to them and declared there was a law or laws in thoes books that I have violated so I better settle and be happy with that. I did and got even with them latter in life.

What is the point of all this jibberish, just this, treat others the way you want to be treated and you will probably stay within the paramiters of the law. Be a wise ass and the boot will catch up to you sooner than you think and it will be your ass that will suffer the most. Take it from one that has had the boot on more than one occasion. Some people never learn from their mistakes. The phrase, "History repeats itself," is very appropriate and is a good partner to, "Past behavior is future performance."

Food for your little brains to think about, laws are designed to punish you, not protect you. The enforcement of law is after you break the law and prevents nothing. Agood example is, why do bars have parking lots when driving under the influence is against the law. How may people drive to the bar for one drink. Ask the angels who were killed by drunken drivers!!!!

RECAP TIME

Congress gives you things and takes them away. Everytime they pass a law your rights are affected. They try to protect the poor and middle class but their efforts are poor. What they don't understand is, it is the poor and the middle class that made rich people rich. RICH PEOPLE DO NOT MAKE RICH PEOPLE RICH AND THEY DO NOT HANG OUT WITH POOR PEOPLE. Don't forget it.

Congress giving to the poor people only makes them poorer. They lose their anbition because someone is handing out to them all the time. When the giving stops they revolt and that is coming down the road. Brats, your not concerned with it now but you will be the adults that have to deal with it latter, good luck.

Stabilize the essentials so their budgets mean something. People on fixed incomes can't make adjustments for gas and food price increases. They can't adjust when energy goes up. They never have an opportunity to save because CONGRESS will keep them POOR and inDEBT forever. The sorry thing about this is the poor are the LAST to see this and the FIRST to feel it. Do the math the numbers don't lie.

Stay informed, it doesn't hurt to know what is going on outside the sports and entertainment world. Remember this and it is simple, CONGRESS CAN'T GIVE YOU ANYTHING THEY DON'T TAKE AWAY FROM YOU OR LATER GENERATIONS. THEY ARE A RECKLESS SPENDING MACHINE AND A BUNCH OF SHEEP.

THE PRESIDENT

What a lazy ass. You can not govern from a desk or a foreign country. The problems that need to be fixed are here in America. Stick your ceremonies where the sun don't shine. A president needs to be out in the field, visiting the different departments that run this country, reviewing management styles and setting goals and getting results.

Should the president be getting first hand knowledge about medicare fraud in the billions or be out lighting a Christmas Tree. Does he know if the person he chose to head the cabinent post knows what the hell their doing or does he wait for a crisis as usual. The latter is the answer.

Why are they signing a bill they have never read. Do you sign documents that way, sure you do because the dam fine print is to long, small and legalized for the average person to understand. The president does the same thing. He doesn't have the balls to tell congress to keep it short, simple and to the point, and they think the more paper they print is job justification. DUMB SHITS.

So now the president get the bill and he signs it. He hasn't read the bill either. The reality is the only one who knows what is in the bill is the one who wrote it and the one who typed it, maybe they should be running the country. It seems the administrative assistants know more than their bosses anyway. If I wanted to know what was going on that's who I would talk to. The bottom line to this is most of the legislation doesn't coinside with common sense, more like no sense, nusience, and non sense.

Like everything in business and in the world, you are only as good as the people you appoint to help you get the job done. The major difference is the business world rewards performance and terminates failure. The government is quite different, they promote you and never monitor your results. They fill a spot and you could die in that spot and no one will ever know or much less care except the person working near you. So what powers does the president really have? This is the falicy, he can veto a bill which means he is smarter than the other 535 congressional people or sign the bill and be as dumb as them. It is a no win situation and everyone will not be happy at the same time.

He is the commander and chief of the military and unless he served he doesn't have a clue what is going on and how they operate, but we give this man the power to make decisions. Here again you are only as smart as the people you surround yourself with. He doesn't even have the balls to tell his wife what to do and he is leading the military. Hoorah!

How dumb is this, he will go and meet foreign leaders and after they reach an accord on an aggrement he must tell them it is dependent on congressional approval. That is like saying you wait til your father gets home and we'll see about this. What he qualifies for is a tour guide and food critic. He can't promise anything that hasn't been budgeted. This is the falicy that the house can only appropriate money, what a crock of crap that is. It is already appropriated in the different budgets for the different agencies. I can imagine the conversation between him and the head of the state department, "Put aside a couple of million for the Russians. I promised them help getting caviar for their social events."

Loopholes, if he knows how to use them he can get a lot accomplished. Just think of the health bill that was passed in 2010, what a joke and a travesty for a democratic country. They leave loopholes in every law or the people are smarter than congress and can always figure out how the get around the law and they do. There is always a wise ass in the bunch.

How much time does he spend on cerimonial horse shit? The only cerimones he should attend are for the military, law enforcement and emergency responders. Let the American people flip the switch on the Christmas tree. These meetings with the world leaders are a joke, what can they solve in two hours. The secretary of state is paid for that job, stay home and work on the problems here.

The real joke is trying to help other countries when everything isn't right at home. Telling other people how to live their live when you don't live in a reasonable society yourself is laughable. I can imagine the other foreign leader thinking, what the hell is he talking about. We have crime, a major drug problem, homeless people, starving people, children be killed in schools, gangs, and a spending habit worse than a drug addict. There is pleanty for the president to do rather than worry about some other countries problems.

The real fact of the matter is he has very little control over his life and what he needs to do to put and keep the country on the right road. He has misguided power lacking precise direction. He needs to run the country from the field and not the seat of his pants sitting at the whitehouse. His job is to get results not sell an idea. Enough about a person without a job description.

OUT OF ORDER BUT ON MY MIND
EDUCATION

What the hell has happened to a system that was at the top of its game. The expression , Dumbing Down America, is very appropriate. There isn't any consistency or standard. Should the federal government be involved at all? What is the direction they are taking and what is with the different grading standards. This no child left behind is a Madison Avenue slogan and nothing more. So what is happening? There are so many board of educations and different authorities and none seem to be going in the same direction. There are students that are smarter than the teachers. There are teachers that can't pass minimum skills test for their job and they are still teaching or is it babysitting. What is the federal government doing? I can tell you, nothing but mucking up the mess that's already out there. The states need to put there foot down and get control. There is too much emphasis on tests and not enough on the skills children need in everyday life. They need to be challenged and the system needs to provide the necessary skills. Children that have difficulty learning and have no mental deficiencies are lazy, not interested or come from families that don't give a damn and use the system to babysit the kids. It starts with the parents and goes to the kids. It works that way in every facit of life. When there are no parents the standard shouldn't change, the solution must be found. Americans are getting dumber as time goes on, according to the people who track this information, and I agree with them

We have more people administering than ever before. It always befuddled my mind why so many educated people needed so many administration people to tell them what to do. I thought educated people need less direction and were better achievers. It doesn't seem that way today. I wonder who the dummies are. Check your mirrors lately.

We need better solutions, simple in nature, and with stringent results. No child left behind is leaving more by the roadside than ever before. We are a nation of mullificaton and no can do attitudes more than ever before. What a tradgey.

Children are not taught how to study.

Children are not taught how to manage their time.

Children are not taught how to manage money.

Children are not taught how to be organized.

Children are not taught responsibility and consequencies for lack of responsibility.

Reading, writing and arithmetic do not teach self reliance. Too many people look to the government for that and that is not their job.

EDUCATION STARTS AT HOME AND NEVERS ENDS.

A side note, your parents have done a great deal in helping you learn and do what is right. Don't think for one minute that you have pulled the wool over Pop Pop, some of you do the least and want the most from it. Well it doesn't work that way. To get 100% you have to give 100% or more. Crap in is crap out, and you will be the dummies. Wake up and keep reading there will be a test later.

POLITICS VERSUS BUSINESS

I'll come right to the point, the wall street assholes are nothing more than a bunch of greedy vacuum cleaners that will suck your hard earned money away from you every chance they get and the government allows this. They are a casino for the big betters to take away money from the occasional betters. In my view 80% of all money invested should be guaranteed or 100% at the banks. Any ceo or cfo that loses more than 15% of risk management money carelessly should go right to jail. Today you will never know what you have to retire on because of the poor management by these banks and brokerage houses. It is insane the amount of money they make for the little they do. The truth of the matter is when they tell you how much they have lost or gained you will never know if they are telling the truth. A fair profit is good, making billions for pushing paper is insane. They will always try to make a buck with someone elses money and the losses are not theirs, they are yours.

Imagine if they took some of the billion they make and gave it to companies to work with for future growth. How much of your investment really makes it to the company you invest in? THE STOCK MARKET IS NOTHING

MORE THAN A GIANT CASINO. The only way I see a company getting their money is on an initial stock offering. People should be able to deal with companies direct to buy their stock with out transfer fees. That should be a cost to the company and there should be limits on trading in that stock as well. That is investing. The more stock Americans as individuals have the more say they should have in how the company is run. We leave it up to the money managers and frankly they have put this country in a financial mess. Their purchasing power is a great weapon against out sourcing, but that will never happen because the manager only cares about how much he makes and what the company makes. He doesn't give a hoot about the small investor and if he has a job tomorrow.

The system is broke and not designed for growth of business or industry. Profit becomes a dirty word when it generates misery.

Marginal buying, day trading, and short sales need to be eliminated. You either own it or you don't. If you want the thrill of making money on a daily basis go to work or bet at a casino, you don't have the right to mess with other peoples money and that is what your doing without their permission. Last of all you shouldn't bet on a company failing. Look in the mirror assholes and what do you see.

This is worth repeating, energy, food and gasoline prices should be stable. Why is it necessary to make a profit from trading this commodity. These are staples in life and your budgets. How can a family do a budget when they never know what the cost of these staples will be, they can't.

Why should they have to cut in their budget just so some ass can make a profit. I am in favor of reasonable profit in these areas. The one thing you never see is a price rollback when the big three go down. They stay the same because you are use to paying them and they fatten the pockets of the companies and what is worst they out source the work so they can make more money. When is enough, enough. Is there a satisfaction level out there?

JOBS LEAVING AMERICA

Why is this? What is the real motivation? Is it the lack of leadership and responsible negotiations with employees? Who comes first, the consumer or the employee? Who got you where you are today?

Why do jobs leave America, because the people at the top don't give a damn about America, they just want what it will give them, more and more and more. Don't kid yourself kiddies, corporate officers don't give a damn about the little guy unless that person can help the reach their goal. Most companies are built by the employees and run by idiots. I say that because in very few cases do they have their money on the line. Not every company is that way but more are, than not.

You must remember, that corporations are like armies, they deal in casualty rates. The companies start with a core group of employees and add to their army. When the generals see an opportunity for bigger profits after a company is on a solid foundation the casualty rate of the employees goes up.They are only interested in today results, not yesterdays history. Companies are starting to see the errors of there ways and offering life time contracts to employees, but that is not at every level. Entry level jobs will always be vulnerable to high risk of termination and cost cutting. Very few companies start cutting at the top.

Now there is a whole bunch of assholes that will tell you about a global economy, but they won't suggest the proper way to operate this economy. It doesn't make sense to send our wealth and hard work overseas. We are ecentually giving ourselves away. We don't make our own phones, light bulbs, and other essentials. This is dumb and has cost America millions of jobs. Most of our manufacturing is outsourced in the name of profit. BULLSHIT.

You sell it here you should make it or assemble it here. This will cost more so it should be built to last longer. The money must stay in this country. The more people who work here the more taxes the government collects and wastes. There needs to be a balance so the people have more to spend on items MADE IN AMERICE. This calls for less taxes and managed spending by the government, wishful thinking, maybe not.

The bottom line to this mess is the little people get hurt and you expand the poorer class to a point of rebellion. I always had a saying that your mothers don't like me to use, so here it is, Shit on me but don't rub my face in it, and that is what the government has been doing.

Out sourcing is a poor excuse for a company to stay alive. The government needs to start putting everyone on a level playing field or we will out source our entire manufacturing base, 50% of it is gone already and the unions are killing the rest. Unions are good for company abuses not employee benefits. What the employees need to realize is they self destruct when they demand more and more. Nothing stands in the way of a greedy Wall Street. Management is also at fault because they don't offer incentives for excellent performance.

Happy employees produce better and more products. So why do we have a greedy Wall Street pushing for profits and a greedy union pushing for benefits and more money. Someday people will learn that certain jobs are only worth certain wages. Auto increases for the same results are destructive. There is always someone who will do it cheaper but not better.

BONUS PAY

Everybody likes more money at the end of the year and I do likewise with our employees. I don't give it for exceptional work but as a gift for Christmas and their loyality to my son and the company. People are paid on a daily basis for their performance and there is a certain level of performance that is expected. The more efficient you work leads to other work and increased compensation. However, if you do the same work every day you should have limits on your compensation. This is never the case, employees always feel entitled to a raise every year. This may be so but they don't consider the increased cost to keep them working or the increase cost of materiale because other companies have to increase the pay of their employees and there costs go up. So, what is the answer down this road to destruction, complicated for sure.

I have always felt that employees be told up front what is expected and what the rewards will be. I also advocate that the rewards are never ending but comesmerate with performance. Today not only do you have to take care of the employees, but students want compensation , as well as children doing choirs and some want renumeration for being good. This is all a crock of crap.

The major flaw here is we all think we can be something better than what we are. That is ok to think that way but reality has to set in. I could never be a rocket scientist but I could be president of the United States. I sure would outperform the current and past presidents. This will probably never happen as I am short in the bullshit department, maybe. My major drawback is I tell people the truth and do what is necessary to get the job done. I don't know any politician who is completely honest, especially these days. So, people have to find where they excell and be happy doing it. There is nothing wrong with just being you and being happy, ask Walt Disney when you see him in the world beyond.

Children should all experience the other side of life, one to give them an appreciation for what they have or to give them an appreciation for what they can achieve. Having survived cancer and seen children with cancer and their love of life and a can do attitude, I can never understand those that have but never think they have enough, and those that do not have and don't have the ambition to do better. This country affords everyone opportunities. I failed in business several times before I was successful. I never stopped trying or dreaming, and I'm still dreaming and I am proud of my successes.

A simple summation is people need to know their limitations and not expect a kings ransom for them. A very difficult comcept to live by. So, when you think you deserve a bonus look in the mirror and be happy with your accomplisments, and what you have that others don't have, that is the best bonus you will ever get.

SMALL BUSINESS, WORKING FOR YOURSELF

I always thought it would be great to work for yourself and I still do. However, I never realized how much we work for the government and the fiscal strangle hold they have on you, not to mention all the regulations they impose on the different industries. They want their money first and you can wait for yours. I remember when we paid our taxes late by one day. I thought they were going to launch a missle at Pop Pops' house. The state is as bad as the federal government. This is why small businessmen like to do cash business, so they can screw the greedy bastards. There is an old saying, a penny saved is a penny earned, or maybe what they really mean is a penny saved is one cheated from someone or something else. The fact of the matter is there are distinct advantages to owning your own business with adherent risks attached to it, government oversight.

Imagine if the government watched themselves as close as they watch small and big business. Imagine the money they would save from doing their job efficiently. Just maybe there wouldn't be a deficit. Wishful thinking!!!! The real fact is, it is better to work for yourself if you have a viable and reciprocal business and if you have management and excellent people skills. Without good skills and people management, you may as well hang it up and go work for a company where your personality isn't a factor. Now if you defuse bombs for a living you would probably want to be left alone to concentrate on your work. What ever the case try to match your skills with your interest and produce work that will make you happy and other people happy. Defusing bombs is not one of those jobs.

EMPLOYEES AND CO WORKERS

There are people you work for, work with, or who work for you. I would prefer to work with or have people work for me. I always treated people that worked for me like I would want to be treated. I never asked someone to do something I haven't done myself or was willing to do myself. I feel you must be fair, firm and honest with people that work for you and with people you will meet throughout your life. This is not a common practice these days.

The people you work with are two dementional, people that really work with you, are loyal and trustworthy, and then there is the phony, hypocritical, beady eyed, back stabbing bastards. Sometimes they are not easy to spot, but eventually they show their stripes and they are not red, white, and blue. Unfortunately for some people it is too late to recover from their affects.

Myself, I would rather work for or with women. They are not as egotistical as men, they are more organized unless you are Amie, they work harder, smarter and very few care about sports at the water cooler. They are a catty bunch at times but I never paid much attention to that. Oh yes, they are much prettier to look at. Yea, I know, you can't say that so you know what I say about that, stick it where the sun don't shine. God didn't put women on this earth to hide. They are here to be adorned, loved and admired for all their achievements and attributes.

Simple, treat people like you want to be treated, be fair in your evaluation, firm in your commitment and consistant with all the people.

MORE ON EDUCATION

Local towns have a board of education that set the tone and give input on ciriculum and look at test results. I just wonder what they are really looking at or are they just concerned with the budget. They follow the money and make the tough decisions on where to cut. Maybe they should pay more attention to why it cost so much in administration cost and teachers salaries. Teachers are paid more if they have masters and doctor degrees, but they are still teaching the same class and getting the same results. There are even situations where the teacher gets reimbursed for extra schooling and paid for the time to go back to school. Where the hell is the oversight here. In Catholic schools an administrator do 10 times the work as public schools according to some report I read several years ago. That being the case I'm sure it is 15 times by now.

Should the federal government be involved at all. What is this nonsense about giving poor communities more money to educate their children. Why does it cost more to teach them or are the teachers inferior? The student lacking discipline will always have a learning problem and they should remain in class til they get it. Leaving dumb is not the answer. Lazy maybe, no motivation, lacking skills, who knows? The fact that they leave for putting in time is a reward to them. Let them stay until they get it and understand it. The reward for going home should be achievement, not failure.

Try this for a while and I am sure you will see the overall grades go up. Infringe on their time rather then them infringing on your time. Classify it under self motivation for self presavation. How can you leave anyone behind that runs for the door when the dismissal bell rings.

LANGUAGE, SWEARING TO BE NOTICED

The primary reason for language is to communicate with each other. The delivery method seems to be the same for everyone. You open your mouth and your brain produces waves that result in sounds and ultimately a language you can understand. So, who do we blame for the foul language, the person, the brain or the mouth. They seem similar to the trinity but I've never heard any foul communication from that direction. I have concluded when someone doesn't want to tell you the truth, or give you the facts, or distract you from the original train of thought, they use a variety of colorful swear words that will get your undevided attention and make you forget the original conversation. Then you have swear words that take the place of adjetives and adverbs because they have multiply meanings. The word fuck has more meanings than all the words in the dictionary. It all depends how you say it and with what reference. Some people say it every other word. This is a good measure of our language skills we were taught in school.

Swear words said in anger have no meaning. They just fill the gap for the brains slow reaction and computation to come up with the right words. Angry people are not rational even though anger in many cases is justified. They are trying to communicate in an hostile enviroment and sometimes it makes that enviroment worse. I have actually heard people use the m fk word in normal conversation in mixed company. Tell me that is not a lack of language skills and improper up bringing. There isn't any excuse to use foul language and I am sure we have all used it normally or in situations of hostility and anger. No one is perfect but your language skills send a clear signal to the people around you about your respect for others and yourself discipline.

Does this indicate I am a goddy too shoes, hell no. I have always tried to express and teach my children the right way. I have impressed on them how it sounds when other people swear. Do they want to sound like that, hell no. Did I ever swear at them, hell yes. Do I correct people when I hear them swear, hell yes. Have I been laughed at for it, yes, and it was clear to me the lack respect they had for me, their family and their friends.

There isn't anyplace in the business world for foul language but it is common from the highest post to the lowest position. I guess the reason it is used a lot is it is easier to build a sentence around a multi meaning word, like the f word. The reality of it is no matter how I think or feel you will be challenged by this behavior as you go through life. Prepare for it, don't fall prey to it and don't be afraid to challenge it.

Pop pop actually read a dictionary one time in my exciting life. It did give me a better understanding of our language, but it hasn't helped my writing skills. I like to write like I think, but I don't always write what I think, lucky you.

What is language without freedom of speech, so they call it. The very few times I see people exercise freedom of speech is when they are angry, then anything goes. When you are angry the brain doesn't have time to find the correct words. It becomes an uncontrollable megaphone. I guess the best way to handle a bad situation is not to get in one. My father always told me never let the other person know what your thinking in an adverse situation, easier said than done. I have blown my gasket on more than one occasion and even in a courtroom. I was asked to never return. I was amazed at the judges' control. My recent tyraids have been with the brats. They come up with some real challenges and they are surprised at my response at times. Enough of this, what is freedom of speech? I really can't tell you because there are words in the English language we can't use because of race, gender and morality. A good example is you are not suppose to use the word nigger in a descriptive emotional way. People are affended by the word, sound, and meaning depending on its' delivery. There is nothing wrong with the word, just how it is used. So the government stepped in and regulated the use of the word. What a crock of shit. A person that uses that word is someone I don't want to be around, white, black, Hispanic, or otherwise. The word is repulsive and I was always told you don't have to be black to be a nigger which is the common meaning. It really signifies a low life and they come in all shapes, colors and sizes, bad is bad. I find the MF word more offensive especially when it is used in mixed company.

Another clueless regulation is comments you make regarding gender. You might say a woman is a hot looking chick, offensive? I think it is the peoson who said it, because if it was said by a person they liked it wouldn't be offensive, it would be cute. Genders use this as an excuse in the work place. If people did their work they wouldn't have time to make dumb comments. This society is to sensitive about themselves and government regulation has helped make it that way. Relax and lighten up, there is nothing that special about you.

Some rules about language,

Don't say it if you don't want it repeated.

Don't say it if you don't want it recorded.

How you say something is just as or more offensive as what you say.

Consider the source if the conversation upsets you.

Think before you respond or put your brain into gear before your mouth goes into motion.

Express yourself in clear, consice words.

Speak at an understandable rythum.

Speak with confidence and conviction.

Sticks and stones will break your bones but words will never hurt you is a crock. They can destroy you, especially if you are a sensitive person and people will see that in you.

Look at a dictionary once in awhile, you will be surprised what you will learn.

Most of all always coverse with respect and You will be treated the same in most situations, if not then you are dealing with a real ignorant asshole. It would be best to avoid this type of person if possible.

Never shy away from a conversation because of a persons intellengce level. You may always learn something even if you don't know what the hell they are talking about. Sometimes they don't know either.

Remember, you will never converse well if you don't learn how to listen to the other person. Eye contact is very important and remember body language.

Always be conscious of what you say and who you say it to.

RESOURCES OF KNOWLEDGE

Lets' face it you can't remember everything, however, you need to have the knowledge where to find the answers for your questions. How to act is not in a book, your parents should have taught you that. It is important for you to use the resources at hand, library, newspapers, magazines, not the kind you see at the grocery store check out, books, and yes the internet. I sure there won't be a short fall in that area.

Try to research subjects, problems, behaviors and many other things before you discuss them with a professional. Prior knowledge is important and you don't have to be an expert, ask opinions and seek legitiment advise. You would not ask a nun how to rob a bank or where could I find a good time in town. Don't ask your mother and father because you never listened to them growing up. I don't see any reason for you to start now, even though they will have your best interest at heart. Sort through the information and keep what makes the most common sense in the situation. You did notice the word common sense, it always works best.

TV and radio are good sources of information but you really need to pay attention to what are the commontaters motives. I will cover this in detail in the next section. You should listen to all the info no matter how slanted it is until you get to the point where it is stupid and ridiculous. If you agree with some of the stupidity you hear or read then your just as stupid as they are. A classic example is when the high courts in California listened to a case regarding illegal alien tuition. What part did they miss about illegal. There is a definent misunderstanding about the word illegal. A good example of this is the president and congressmen swear to uphold the constitution. Do they do this. It is becoming a joke and they will be the first to tell you they don't pay any attention to the constitution and that is probably the most accurate statement they will ever make.

When you listen to a politician and you are confused afterward, don't worry, that is normal. They have an innate ability to bullshit around the conversation or issues and still smile at you while they turn the screws. If you hear them answer yes or no to a question it will be a first. They probably even lie about their age.

When you solicitate information you have to be the best judge of what makes the most sense. You will either celeberate the rewards of your decision or suffer the consequencies and there are always consequiencies.

MEDIA, WHO DO YOU BELIEVE

Just to put you in the right mood for this conversation you need to know you can lie about your military service, because the supreme court stated it was ok to lie. The one thing you need to know about lying is you will always eventually get caught. If your not man or woman enough to face up to your short comings, don't lie, it would be best not to say anything.

I always listened to Imus in the Morning. He doesn't have any agenda other than to make people laugh, embarrass his guess into telling the real truth, or put a guess on the spot where they have to tell you the truth. It is fun to listen to and informative because he doesn't care what their affiliations are he just wants to have a good time. The other reason I enjoy listening to him is as rich as he is he can still relate to his audience at every level. I don't always agree with everything he says but I know it is never meant to be malicious, just humorous.

He can be a real sissy boy at times but he is there when the chips are down, ask any of the children he puts through the ranch. He has a heart of gold and mush for brains but I'll stand by him anytime. No, I have never meant the man but I do admire him. You need to look past the shock jock label and realize that it is informative entertainment. Going through life without laughter is like being water boarded, waiting for the next drop. Imus provides laughter that helps keep you going and we all know laughing is good for the soul. What you really have to keep in mind is that it is ok to laugh at yourself with others. Look in the mirror every morning and smile, you will see a different person and you might like them.

There are other personalities that provide solid information but they have an agenda and it is this way on both sides. You must learn to listen to everyone. The best way to know what the opposition is doing is listen to them. There delivery is based on fear and depression. Seldom do I ever hear them offer solution other than vote the bastards out. Regardless, they do provide important conflicting information, use it wisely.

My afternoon is occupied with Tom Sullivan of Fox. He is reasonable, listens' and responds with intelligence. He Doesn't have some of the entertainment value as others but he delivers the important message and never insults his listeners. He and Imus are a credit to their industry. You need to listen to a persons heart to know what they are about.

FINANCIAL RESPONSIBILITY

I am the last person you should be talking to about this, but I have learned my lesson well, so pay attention. Financial responsibility starts when you learn what money can do for you and do TO YOU. The premise that you can work off a budget is fesible to a point but mostly a crock of crap. It is very difficult to be on a budget when basic cost of living keep going up and down at the whim of the greedy bastards on wall street and the do nothing government.

Simple money management would be don't spend it if you don't have it. Too simple to understand, try this, only pay cash for your purchases. Still don't understand then get someone to manage your money for you because your to damn dumb and you are an impulse buyer. Simple.

UNDERSTAND THIS AND DON'T FORGET, THE GOVERNMENT WILL NOT BE ABLE TO PROVIDE FOR YOU WHEN YOU ARE READY TO RETIRE. SOCIAL SECURITY WILL BE NON EXISTENT. PLAN FOR YOUR FUTURE.

The government has spent your future and is still spending more. They are a sick bunch with their own personal interest at heart. They think for the moment and not for the future and they could really care less about you except at voting time. I remember meeting the governor of New Jersey at a social event and he said he remembered me from other events. What a crock, that was our only meeting and I'm glad he is gone from the political scene. The point is, do not depend on the government for any help.

Credit is for emergencies or making long term purchases on big ticket items such as homes and cars. It is not for everyday items. The debit card is good for that. You will see the day when all you will have is a debit card to make purchases. Cash will be a thing of the pass but while we still have it there are some rules you must follow.

1. Pay yourself first. Put a certain amount of money in savings. If you invest in stock or funds then make sure you are getting a dividend. If you put $50.00 dollars away a week you should only put 10% or 5.00 into high risk investments. The 90% should be in conservative investments.
2. Save separately for vacations. Everyone needs time away with family or by yourself. Don't tap savings, it should be a separate fund and if you can only afford time away every two years get the most for your money and make it memorable. You can't live on dreams but you can work toward them.
3. Before you make an important purchase, research and research more.
4. Try to live by a budget but remember to have enough for fluctuations.
5. Reconcile your finances every month. Make sure they balance and be very aware of new charges or suspicious activity in your accounts.

6. Protect your passwords and valuables. Free information is dangerous information. Idle conversation in public about your finances is dangerous.

7. Seek professional help when you are not sure in a financial decision. Don't be afraid to ask for references and performance results.

8. You must watch your investments. The people who sold you on a particular investment are sales people and they spend their time selling more investments not watching your portfolio. Check daily.

9. Don't be asking Pop Pop for any money. What I give for free is advise.

10. Shop for a home mortgage like you shop for food. Get the best value for your money. Review all cost and fees associated with a mortgage. If there is a builders clause in the contract that states they will receive 1% of the seeing price of a home evrytime the property changes hands, do not buy it. This is a hidden cost that is in the deed on the property. Always ask about it and view all answers with caution. Salespeople will tell you anything because they are to lazy to look for the answer. They make money selling, not researching. Like everything else there is good and bad.

11. School loans, I guess the government took care of that. They are the lender and they will become the collector if you miss your payments and they will lock up your accounts and garnish you wages. They are ruthless. Everyone business is ruthless when it comes to money. You must protect and be

aware at all times when it comes to your money and investments.

12. Above all, EDUCATE YOURSELF AND RESEARCH before you make your decisions. It is your future and we won't be around to HELP.

I HOPE YOU GET THE POINT. When you have to work for the money you will understand this a little better. You must be self sufficient.

HEALTH CARE

Pop Pop did not do the best job in this area. The Vietnam war didn't help either, but I made a decision to volunteer my service to my country and I would do it over again.

Information was not as available 50 years ago like it is today. Your situation in life lead you to poor choices at times and the botton line to that is you will pay for it somewhere in the future. If you punish your body because of poor eating habits, wanted or unwanted, you will suffer later. You can take that to the bank, it will happen.

Who ever coined the phrase , "YOU ARE WHAT YOU EAT," was right on the money. What you eat has an immediate affect on your mood, intelligence, and your mobility. Ther isn't much you can do while your sleeping from over eating.

Thin might be in but Fat where its at is a crock of fat. FAT IS DANGEROUS. There isn't any scientific data that defends fat unless you're a bear hibernating. We sleep a third of our life and we need to do this so the body can reward itself for the good nutrition or repair itself from the bad nutrition and abuse. The main ingredient in good healt and nutrition is WILL POWER AND DISCIPLINE.

Without these strong and necessary traits life will be a

difficult road for anyone. I have been up and down that road too many times. I can't tell you how to get will power and discipline except to tell you it comes from good daily habits. They are important in all aspects of your life and are major contributors to your success. You only have one body, take care of it.

DRUGS

We have drugs to help with our deficiences in caring for ourselves and other diseases out of our control. The less you take the better off you are. The food you eat, if properly, will give you all the nourishment you need to sustain a healthy lifestyle. Pescription drugs are necessary when the body needs help and not to be used as a way of life. Be very careful as they can kill you over the long haul. They don't put warnings on them for nothing.

Other drugs, such as entertainment enhancers, are habit forming, extremely dangerous and clear evidence of your lack of control or individuality. They are sending a message that you are weak minded. There isn't any sane excuse for there abuse and the misery it causes to our society. They are a cheap form of entertainment and exhibition.

People who use drugs are as responsible as the people who supply, sell, and commit crimes in there operations. If you consider using them, think about the innocent people who have died along the way in the process to get this drug to you. Yes these social and hardcore drug users are as guilty as the people who kill for their profit from this product. LOOK AT

IT AND ASK YOURSELF HOW MANY PEOPLE DIED ALONG THE WAY.

If you succumb to peer pressure to use drugs, remember this, real friends never hurt each other, you have to decide what kind of friend you want to be. If you ever make that decision and I find out I will put a hurting on you that Medicare won't cover. You will carry that scar as a reminder when you fall from grace. This is a promise.

That said, I can tell you I tried pot when I was in Vietnam. I can tell you that you do lose your senses and your ability to control yourself and don't let anyone tell you otherwise. They are lying to you and have other motives. You are not a safe person when you are on drugs and you are very capable of hurting others. That is unacceptable.

Drinking is as bad as drugs when you abuse it. Smoking is sucking in chemicals you wouldn't put on your dinner plate. They are all a waste of money and do destroy the body over time or in some cases kill you immediately. That is like in DEAD, gone from this world forever. Your decision, but put this image in your mind of Pop Pop beating the hell out of you, and when I get too old I 'll find someone who can. Enough said.

Drinking is nothing more than dressing up acohol so it taste good. That is what a good chef does when the food is bland, he adds ingredients that make it taste good. Drinking and anything you do don't mix. You don't have control of yourself and you can hurt other people. If you are at a social event, a drink is responsible, two drinks is stupid and three drinks will have people talking and laughing at you. The decision you have to make is do you want to be a part of the conversation or about the conversation.

Health care companies are not in business to lose money.

This is a cost that will never go down and the one cost you have some control over, not smoking and drinking are a plus. You must be very aware of what the companies will and will not cover. You can be dropped like a hot potato at any time if it suit's the company. Protect yourself as best you can. Make no mistake about it, we all get sick at some point in our life, taking care of yourself gives you the best chance of recovery.

RESPONSIBILITY

Accepting responsibility for your own actions is difficult to do for most people. They have excuses why they can't do things, lack of courage to hone up to their failures and mistakes, and most of all lack of honesty to themselves. You are not going through life with a perfect result. There will be successes, failures, disappointments,and achievements. They all come with the responsibility of taking credit or suffering the defeat. Lets' face it none of us likes to lose or admit they might be to cause for the loss. These episodes in life are called learning experiences. They come with a price, positive or negative. The key is to learn from them and benefit from the experience down the road. If you keep running into a brick wall in life, I hope you have enough sense left to seek help.

It is easy to let the other person do it while you sit in a safty zone. That is what most people do, especially politicans. They have difficulty doing anything and admitting they are wrong. Often we discuss the state of America and the problems we face as a nation. Too often it is pushed to the side for more pleasurable conversation. People are afraid to stand by their convictions. It is easier to blame someone else for your problems but never give them credit for your conforts.

This society has an entitlement mentality. They think they are owed something and to some degree they are right, especially the people paying into social security. They did not envision the congress spending their retirement. They didn't get involved when it mattered and now they have to pay the price and they don't want too. Lets face it we are all responsible to some degree, no mistake about that. The world owes you nothing. Your parents have given to you most of your life and you still want more. The bank is empty so you have to take care of yourself, which means, starting now. You will have to pay the debt your parents built for you because they neglected their responsibility. You will have to pay the price for, we don't talk politics, because the politicians do and look what they have done for you.

What is being responsible, being liable for your own actions or inactivity because the matter was to sensitive to talk about. Being passionate about something and waiting for the next person to lead the way. Saying I did that. Challenging stupidity and dishonesty. There are so many ways to be and not to be responsible, the key is looking into the mirror and seeing something you like, knowing that you are your own person.

This is what you are entitled to, living as a decent, kind, respectful human being. You are entitled to treatment in kind. You are entitled to a good education and competent care until you are of age. After that the world owes you nothing and don't expect it. Good luck.

1/8/2011 CONGRESS WOMAN SHOT AND OTHERS KILLED

This is without a doubt a despicable act by a sick individual. It received mega media coverage because it happened at a political event. The media turned it into a circus and tried to spin it in every direction. What it amounted to was a clear case of the local, state and federal government failure. There were warning signs all along the way that received no credible response at any level. The results were innocent people were killed and injured. What is clear is the lack of responsibility accepted by all. What does this have to with this incident, it could have been prevented.

I stated before that America doesn't have an identity of its' own. Everyone wants to be someone else or something and American. The congress, after 235 years hasn't passed a common language law, hasn't passed restrictions on burning the American Flag, hasn't passed minimun requirements regarding citizenship and hasn't made it clear to all the people who come to this country that you will be Americans or stay home and be what you want to be. This of cultural celebrations in this country should be eliminated. Are you an American or not? Who will you expect help from when a disaster or medical problems occur. I am sure you will not run back to your parents or your point of origin. This country lacks strict rules for citizenship and doesn't enforce the rules we have. That is why they are partly responsible for the tradgedy in Arizona. They cater to special groups.

This is not America when all you hear is republican, democrat and independent rant on what is wrong. Maybe we should call this country RID, because they are constantly pursuing their own agendas and not thinking of America. Maybe we should get rid of RID altogether vote in congress people from a list of possible canidates based on their QUALIFICTIONS. Just maybe that would help this government run something right and efficiently. We have not been successful in any agency that I am aware of, especially the irs.

This country faces may domestic and foreign challengces, but the number one chalengce is our own identity. Diversity within our boarders does not work, we have proved that. Radical culture differences cause too much controversy and animosity. People hate us because of the way we live and we hate each other because of the way we live together. Any culture, religion, activist groups or anti government movement should be banned and outlawed. I don't care what the aclu thinks. The founding fathers didn't give us these rights to practice and hurt other people and hide behind the law. That was not their intent and I will argue that point with anyone.

So for my grandchildren, never be afraid or concerned with what other people think. When asked, proudly state that you are American, born and raised in the greatest country in the world. If you do not see American on any applications you fill out, then write it in. You are not Italian, black, white, hispanic, European, catholic, jewish, muslin, christian and so on. YOU ARE AMERICANS first and that is what gives you the opportunity to be what ever you want to be and never forget it. If government did what was right for the people, this incident would never have happened

MILITARY SERVICE

There was a day when you couldn't do anything right your parents told you to join the military. They just wanted you to have a new mother and father. The military is strict discipline and rules. Do what they say, how they say and when they say, especially when we were at war or engaged in a police action. They did not always get the cream of the crop.

Today, the picture is quite different. They only want the cream of the crop with some average achievers to do the mundane duties. You need both to operate efficiently. Pop Pop volunteered for the Marine Corp after I was rated one Y. This was because I had bad vision in one eye and weighed 300 lbs. The vision was the major drawback. During a time when the chicken shits were running to the border, I prompted my congress woman at the time to exert some pressure to get me in and she did and I immediately regretted it within 45 seconds of getting off the bus at Parris Island. It just wasn't like the movies portrayed it. To keep it short, I volunteered for Vietnam and I'm still here writing this book.

Never be afraid to serve your country in some form of service. Just to keep the record straight, even though I dislike the politicans, I think they make their job a thankless job.

They are in a can't please everyone enviroment so they please themselves and their cronies the most. If you ever go that route in life and become like them instead of doing what is right for America, CHANGE YOUR NAME. Don't plead the case I'm doing what my constiuants want, because if they want something for themselves then they are no better than the people they send into office. This is America.

Understand one important fact about life and the military, there is always someone who outranks you and will give you orders. You say how can that be, get married and you will find out. This is the chain of command in life, children, mother, father, grand parents, or wife, husband. This is in the majority of families these days and persistence dictates.

In the military you start at the bottom and you must realize there is no top. You will always have a boss, ask General Douglas Mc Arthur. Bosses graduate in different ranks and your future is always in someone elses hand. They don't like you and you go no where. This is the same in the business world, only they put it a different way, what have you done for me TODAY. The phrase, history belongs in history books, and that is where past performance belongs also.

About discipline, a part of life you reject unless it serves your purpose, you have very little at this point in your life. You are good at doing the routine and mundane things in your life, but when it comes to change, the battle lines are drawn. The military doesn't give you a vote or a voice. Objection is not a word in the military dictionary, objective is. If you feel for any reason you can't follow direction, don't join, serve in another way. There is nothing worse than going through part of your life miserable. If you are drafted, make the best use of your time in service to improve yourself and GOOD LUCK.

WHAT PART OF THIS DON'T YOU UNDERSTAND

I COULD GO ON FOREVER BUT I WON'T. Your little minds must absorb what you read, remember what will benefit you, and put into action what you will have to do to survive and have a successful and respectful life. I sincerely hope your generation is more responsible than mine has been. When we say I'm doing it our children, what really comes out is we did it to our children. So know this with all your heart, POP POP loved you dearly, disciplined you wisely, treated you fairly, and will continue to do so for the remainder of my existence in this great nation of ours, AMERICA.

So, what part of this don't you understand, in no particular order:

1. Don't spend more than you have and send that message to the government.
2. Respect is earned, it is not a God given right.
3. Treat others the way you want to be treated and if they take advantage of you return the jesture 10 times over.
4. Never let people take advantage of small children or

beat them without you taking some kind of action to help them. Children are not punching bags.

5. People will only do to you what you let them do to you.

6. Responsibility is something you accept not forego.

7. Never be afraid to admit a mistake, just don't repeat it.

8. Don't wait for the other guy to do it.

9. Remember there will be people in your life who don't like you, don't be afraid of them and don't let them take advantage of you.

10. Never change your beliefs to accommodate others.

11. Think about all the things you can do and have a can do attitude.

12. If you have an attitude, lose it. I will cause you more than trouble.

13. Don't follow the crowd. Make up your own mind.

14. If you can't make up your own mind, stay home with your parents. They will lead you in the right direction.

15. Abide by the house rules. The king of the house make the rules.

16. The king is the one who pays the bills.

17. Be happy, it is a lot easier than living miserable.

18. Be a realist, but never stop dreaming. As long as the glass is half full you will have the opportunity to fill it all the way. Can Do.

19. Don't be afraid to ask questions and say you don't know.

20. Remember small minds never see big pictures.

21. Think outside the box and look for possibilities.

22. There is nothing more important than education. Never stop learning and never be afraid to teach.

23. The government owes as much as the gross national product. We have no surplus which means we are bankrupt as a nation. Crime, civil disobedience and maybe another recession or depression will follow. People will not be nice. Know that change will come and you won't like it.

24. Talk to your parents about the state of affairs. It may be boring to you now but the day may come when they tell you they can't afford to send you to college, then it will hit home.

25. Remember that family is more important than tradition and heritage. The latter two can't help you, only family can.

26. Never give up on America. It did not create this mess, people did.

27. Disagreement is not a licence to carry anger or revenge. Discussion and disagreement is good in the right enviroment.

28. Speak your own mind, and don't be a parrot.

29. Faith and hope will carry you a lot further than dispare and doubt.

30. How you see the glass is not as important as what you do with it.

31. Set a fiduciary example and advise your congress people to follow. Get involved and communicate with them. They need all the help they can get.

32. Recognising problems is not as good as finding solution for them.

33. Pass this book along to your peers.

34. Listen to what adults have to say and judge for yourself if it makes sense. If you don't understand, ask questions.

35. Don't be a hypocrit and don't put yourself in a position to be one.

36. Take care of your body, its not like your teeth, you don't get a second one.

37. The best medicine is preventive, when it goes pass that point trust your doctor but use your resources to be informed.

38. Drugs and acohol kill when abused and kill over the long haul. They don't print warning labels for nothing, that is if you can read them.

39. Did you ever wonder why it cost so much money to elect a president who will spend so much money.

40. Congress spends your money, the senate stamps the check and the president signs it.

41. How come congress never knows how much they spend until its to late?

42. Small minds never see big pictures or true reflections.

43. The president advises Americans to act responsibly. Sounds great except they never set the example to follow.

44. Did you ever hear the expression, read it before you sign it, what part of that did congress and the president miss.

45. If it doesn't affect you directly, don't worry about it. It will catch up to you later.

47. If you believe everything you hear, see and read, then you must have graduated Harvard.

48. If you believe everything you say or repeat, then you must have graduated Princeton.

49. If you believe everything you read in this book, then you should be teaching at Harvard and Princeton.

50. Respect all the military, police, fire, and emergency people. They risk their life every day to maintain a sane world. They are not mind readers so they can't look into a crystal ball to prevent crime. If you don't look for trouble it won't find you, but always be aware.

51. Don't ever take God for granted, you just didn't happen and it didn't take a million years for you to evolve.

52. Learn how to forgive but don't ever forget, good or bad.

53. Do you know what coupons are, then you better learn.

54. Banks and lawyers are only good when you need them and they charge large fees. Everything comes with a price tag. You did when you were born and your parents didn't mind paying the bill. I hope they never have to regret it. I never have.

This list could go on forever, but it is easy to complain about the problems. What you need are solutions and I will give you my thoughts on that as well, aren't you lucky.

HERE COME THE SOLUTIONS

The cost of fuel and fuel for heat are higher than your food bills. The electric car is suppose to help solve that problem, but the use of natural gas is a better solution. You still have to burn coal and oil for electric and what do you do when the power goes out. No car for emergencies? Just think of riding down the road and the battery goes dead like it does in your cell phone. Maybe they will have outlets on the road like they had phone booths. To lower the price of gas:

1. Enforce the speed limit. Let the speeders fines pay part of the deficit.
2. Reduce the speed limits.
3. Maximise engine horsepower.
4. Reduce acceleration rates.
5. Do away with drive thrus. The exercise won't hurt.
6. Do away with toll booths.

Saving fuel for energy:

1. Use motion sensors to turn off lights not used for security.
2. Build and insulate properly.

3. Install instant hot water heaters and do away with tanks where possible.
4. Install supply lines on inside walls as much as possible.
5. Insulate duct work better.
6. Install multi speed motors and have reduced heat modes.
7. Reduce duck work size and have more supplies.
8. Make the home positive.

Saving on food cost:
1. Use coupons.
2. Reduce delivery expenses, gas prices.
3. Increase inspections and reduce recalls.
4. Eat less, we can all do that.
5. Take advantage of all the sales, buy extra on really low prices.
6. Shop like you are on your last penny, value.
7. Don't bump into the old people with your cart, they will get even.
8. Use your debit card, not your credit card, to pay.
9. Stay the hell out of the junk food isle, yeah right.

National solutions can't help if you don't establish a common language and make it mandatory to learn the language. The people must be as one. Celebrating anything other than the Forth of July is counter productive. Allowing a law to burn the American flag in protest is promoting diversity and not unification. That is what the Civil War was all about, remember. Stop promoting separation based on heritage and the color of peoples skin. Think of America first and lead by setting an example, and stop minding other countries business. Bring home the military and stop fighting cultural wars.

There must be a different mindset in congress.

1. Congress, don't spend more than you have. People will not miss what government does not provide, so stop providing.

2. Reduce the size of government and put a freeze on hiring. Spread the work out as people retire or die. This is what a family does when someone moves on or passes away. The responsibilities are spread amoung other family members or assumed by the survivor. Get it dummies.

3. Reduce travel expenses.

4. Don't pass legislation you can't read or have the average American understand. KEEP IT SIMPLE STUPID.

5. No more earmarks.

6. No more federal employee bonus.

7. Reduce agriculture subsidies, why are we paying tabbaco subsidies when the product kills people and increases our health care cost. DAH!

8. The military needs to operate more efficiently. Less outside contractors.

9. Stop mandating laws the states can not afford. If the federal government can't pay for it then don't do it.

10. THERE MUST BE A FLAT TAX WITHOUT DEDUCTIONS AND A FEDERAL TAX ON TOP EARNERS AND DON'T GIVE ME THIS BULLSHIT ABOUT THEY GENERATE JOBS. Necessity generates jobs and I don't know

any business man who will hire someone that will reduce their bottom line except the government.

11 **Run the government like a business and treat the tax payers as stock holders**. Deficits are not an option.

12. Start a national lottery to pay off the deficit. Have multiple one million dollar winners without taxes deducted.

13. The government should provide mortgages to all serving and retired military personell. The interest should be low and the interest on the loans should go toward helping the veterns and paying part of the national debt.

14. Close the boarders and legalize the the illegal aliens with restriction on citizenship for their actions.

15. Make it against the law for any religion or group to be governed by law contrary to American law.

16. Make it a law that if it is sold in America, that the parts should be made in America or assembled in America. Trade deficits are couter productive and it is not Americas' job to provide to the rest of the world but to HELP when necessary.

17. The federal government needs to set a minimun standard for education and then get out of the business of education. That is a problem better served by the state and the people of that state.

18. Set a mandatory furlough for all non essential government employees. This will include the congressional staff and whitehouse staff.

19. Renigotiate all civil service contracts so they make sense.

20. Cut mail service to five days a week. We still survive when we don't get mail on the holidays.

21. Put a heavy tax on all deals that sell our technology to foreign governments.

22. Arrest on a daily basis if necessary all drug users that snort, smoke, inject or otherwise take illegal drugs with a minimun fine of five hundred dollars, 80% of which will go directly to deficit reduction. Their habits have caused more deaths on the supply and user side and been responsible for loss production in the work force.

23. All drug users and achololics that receive disability benefits should be put in restricted living quarters and provided the essentials of life. They should not receive money from the social security fund. America doesn't need to support bad habits with taxpayers money.

24. Every one receiving a government check or fund transfer should be charged a $1.00 fee to be applied to the deficit. This includes all government employees and excludes serving military.

25. The government should have a no gun list similar to a no fly list. Weapons should not be sold over the internet. This should include all mental patients and patients receiving drugs for mental disorders.

26. The NRA association should prequalify all potential gun owners before they purchase a weapon.

27. People should be issued a computerized health card from birth that will interface with all legal medical facilities and doctors. This will help prevent duplicate testing and mutual care.

28. All medical personell who receive medicare

and Medicaid payment should apply in person and be fingerprinted. All documentation should be authenticated in person especially place of business.

29. The government should tax every uninsured person. This money should go into a fund for first time users. Once a person draws from this fund for a visit or hospitalazation, they should be required to have health insurance at some level.

30. All insurance companies should cover all medical conditions from birth to death. All agencies should share in catastrophic costs and treatments.

31. All reasonable medical bills should be paid according to a patients ability to pay. Medical bills are like taxes, you pay til you die. You can't legislate responsibility but you can tax and fine their lack of responsibility.

32. Abortions shoul be illegal unless it is a medical emergency.

33. All reciepiants of welfare or assistance should be prepared to work at the governments request at local, state and federal levels. In other words, only hitch hikers get a free ride.

34. There should be a mandatory financial responsibility class taught at elementary and high school levels. There will be no failing of this class and it will be repeated until it is passed at 80% level. Failure is not an option.

35. If we are going to teach by following an example, then we shouldn't use the government as the example to follow. They receive a failing grade so

they shouldn't get a wage increase. They should give some money back.

36. People that never paid taxes should not have the right to vote. Freedom comes at a cost whether it is blood or money. People that don't contribute should not decide how the money is spent or who will lead the country. This is the most flagrant violation of taxes without representation.

37. People should be given a short quiz at the poling booth to determine if they really know what they are doing or are they responding like a dog waiting on a treat.

38. Being able to read English should be a requirement for voting.

39. Spending billions on elections should be against the law. Candidates should have debates in many different forums. Candidates should be elected on their merit not their money.

40. Congress should not police itself. A civilian review board should be elected to serve per case like jury duty.

I could go on forever but it means nothing unless people are willing to sacrifice and volunteer to put the country back on track for world leader status by example. We, as a country, need to mind our business more and others less. We have been shit on by our own government and now they are rubbing our faces in it. The question we will need to answer is how much are we willing to sacrifice. I am afraid of the answer.

The nation needs to stop exporting its wealth for the sake of others. We don't seem to relize that we can't export our money and try to help others at the same time. We are in more debt than any other nation and the well is running dry.

We are a spoiled nation and I can see why other nation are looking down on us. We are in a decline on every level except borrowing money. Education is sliding and a clear measure of this is the number of people we have that can't read. Another indication is our lack of financial responsibility and waste at every level of government. Giving money to other nations and knowing that most of it goes toward corruption and waste is a clear example of rubbing our face in it. The simple process would be to supply the parts and service that is needed to help the other nations, not give them a blank check.

This is the bottom line, get involved at some level. Stay informed about you local, state, and federal governments. Our generation worked and waited for the other guy to do it. That doesn't work in this era. People will label you because it is easier to do that then help resolve the problem. The governments answer to everything is to waste money on it and we proved that will not work. Greed and corruption will follow the average hard working people to their graves and the message will be clear, leave it for the next generation, but there is nothing left for that generation to work with except sacrifice, dispare, and civil unrest that will follow. You will truly need the protection of the second amendment, the right to bear arms. I just hope the right people have those weapons and know how to protect themselves.

A critical mistake at this point is to let the people who caused the problem solve the problem. This isn't going to happen. When the money runs dry and it will, tempers will fly and the blame game will start all over again. This is why we all need the same identity, without this the different groups will blame each other and they will never believe what needs to be done will be fair to all. This country has to have a different mindset about itself. They need to stop preaching the poor against the rich and the ethnic groups against each other. Poor is poor no matter what your background is. They will suffer first and most. The government can't be a provider for anyone when it can't provide for itself. All they keep doing is extending the crisis and making it worse.

You will probably be happy that I will end on this note, you will have to provide for you and your families. You can't do this with empty pockets so remember the first rule is to save for the future, you will need it. The next rule is don't hurt anyone else on your way to success and financial security. Honest earnings are the best earnings and you get that through hard work and filling the glass up. Educating yourself is important, but using that education is more important. Always remember that small minds never see big pictures.

GOOD LUCK, I HOPE YOU READ MY THOUGHTS BEFORE IT IS TOO LATE.

LOVE AND GOD BLESS US ALL, POP POP.

CATEGORIES

FIXING AMERICA FOR THE GRANDCHILDREN
BORN IN AMERICA, SO WHAT ARE YOU
NO COMMON LANGUAGE OR HERITAGE
WHO BELONGS IN AMERICA
THE AMERICAN FLAG
THE CONSTITUTION OF THE UNITED STATES OF
AMERICA
RECAP TIME
POWER TO THE PEOPLE
CONGRESS, HOW DOES CONGRESS WORK,
ACTUALLY IT DOESN'T
WHAT IS LEGISLATION DESIGNED TO DO
PROTECT YOU AND THE COUNTRY
MONEY, MONEY AND MORE MONEY
WHO SHOULD PAY TAXES
THE MORE THEY LEGISLATE THE MORE RIGHTS
YOU GIVE UP
RECAP TIME
THE PRESIDENT
OUT OF ORDER BUT ON MY MIND, EDUCATION
POLITICS VERSUS BUSINESS

JOBS LEAVING AMERICA
BONUS PAY
SMALL BUSINESS, WORKING FOR YOURSELF
EMPLOYEES AND CO WORKERS
MORE ON EDUCATION
LANGUAGE, SWEARING TO BE NOTICED
RESOURCES AND KNOWLEDGE
MEDIA, WHO DO YOU BELIEVE
FINANICAL RESPONSIBILITY
HEALTH CARE
DRUGS
RESPONSIBILITY
1/8/2011 CONGRESSWOMAN SHOTAND OTHERS KILLED
MILITARY SERVICE

WHAT PART OF THIS DON'T YOU UNDERSTAND

HERE COMES THE SOLUTIONS

THE END

SAVING AMERICA AND OUR GRANDCHILDREN